THE MARY CELESTE

BY KIMBERLY ZIEMANN

Apex is distributed by North Star Editions:
sales@northstareditions.com | 888-417-0195

Produced for Apex by Red Line Editorial.

Photographs ©: The History Collection/Alamy, cover; AP Images, 4–5; Chronicle/Alamy, 6; Shutterstock Images, 8–9, 20, 21, 29; iStockphoto, 9, 12–13; Detroit Publishing Company/Library of Congress, 10–11; Wikimedia, 14; The Miriam and Ira D. Wallach Division of Art/New York Public Library, 15, 19; Library of Congress, 16–17; Armstrong & Co./Library of Congress, 1, 22–23; National Park Service, 24; Arnold Genthe/Genthe Photograph Collection/Library of Congress, 27

Library of Congress Control Number: 2022911841

ISBN
978-1-63738-435-0 (hardcover)
978-1-63738-462-6 (paperback)
978-1-63738-514-2 (ebook pdf)
978-1-63738-489-3 (hosted ebook)

Printed in the United States of America
Mankato, MN
012023

NOTE TO PARENTS AND EDUCATORS

Apex books are designed to build literacy skills in striving readers. Exciting, high-interest content attracts and holds readers' attention. The text is carefully leveled to allow students to achieve success quickly. Additional features, such as bolded glossary words for difficult terms, help build comprehension.

TABLE OF CONTENTS

CHAPTER 1

GHOST SHIP

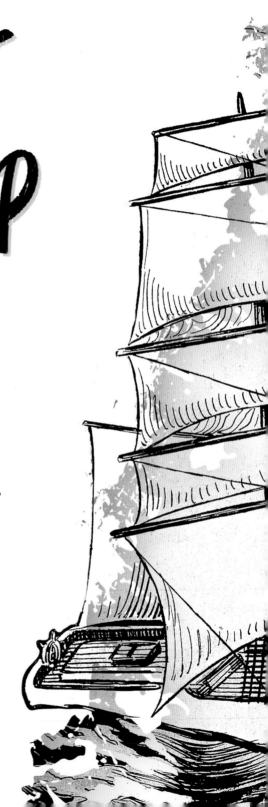

On December 5, 1872, sailors saw something strange. They spotted another ship at sea. It seemed to be in trouble.

The *Mary Celeste* was a brigantine. This type of ship has two masts.

The ship flew only a few torn sails. The name on the ship was the *Mary Celeste*. The sailors rowed over. No one was found on board.

◀ **A woodcut shows sailors boarding the *Mary Celeste*.**

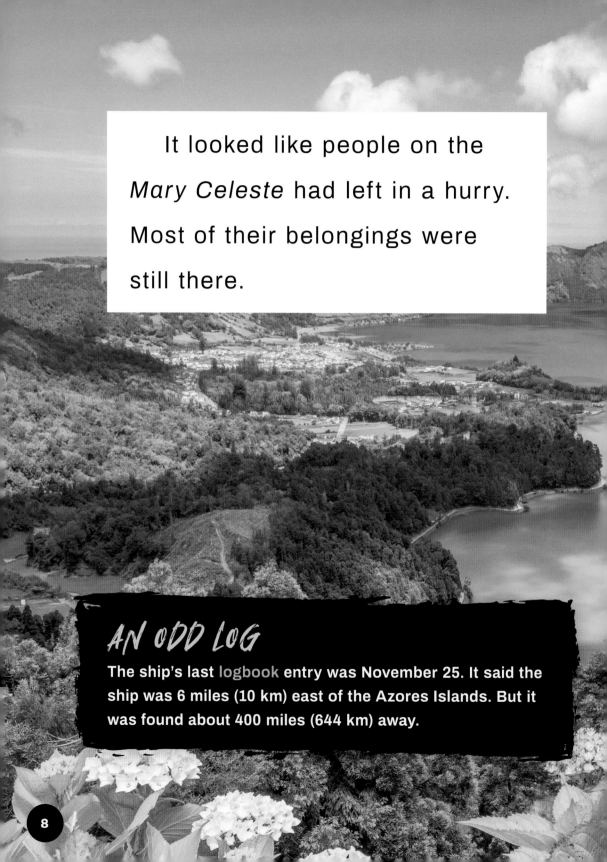

It looked like people on the *Mary Celeste* had left in a hurry. Most of their belongings were still there.

AN ODD LOG

The ship's last logbook entry was November 25. It said the ship was 6 miles (10 km) east of the Azores Islands. But it was found about 400 miles (644 km) away.

The Azores Islands are in the Atlantic Ocean. They are about 1,000 miles (1,600 km) west of Portugal.

The last logbook entry was 10 days before sailors found the ship. People wondered what happened.

CHAPTER 2

A CURSED SHIP?

Some people said the *Mary Celeste* was cursed. The captain got sick on its first trip. He died.

Brigantines like the *Mary Celeste* often had crews of about 10 to 20 people.

The second captain got
caught in a strong storm.
The ship became stuck on a
rocky shore.

The *Mary Celeste* was built in Nova Scotia. The area was known for shipbuilding and fishing.

CHANGING NAMES

Workers built the ship in 1861. Its first name was the *Amazon*. The ship was sold in 1868. The new owner named it the *Mary Celeste*.

The *Mary Celeste*'s third captain was Benjamin Briggs. He set sail on November 7, 1872. His wife and daughter joined him. Seven other sailors came, too. None were ever seen again.

Benjamin Briggs was from the US state of Massachusetts.

The *Mary Celeste* set sail from the harbor of New York City.

FAST FACT

Captain Briggs left his son behind. The boy stayed with his grandmother so he wouldn't miss school.

CHAPTER 3

MYSTERIES

nvestigators tried to find out what had happened. Some people thought pirates had attacked. But there was no evidence of fighting. And nothing was stolen.

Some people thought pirates had made everyone on the *Mary Celeste* walk the plank.

Others thought a storm had washed everyone overboard. But people found clothes on the ship. Sailors would have worn those clothes in stormy weather.

A BLOODY SWORD?

Investigators found a sword on the *Mary Celeste*. The sword had dark marks. They thought the marks were blood. But they were only bits of iron.

Sailors wore oilskins during stormy seasons. These clothes kept them dry.

The ship also carried industrial alcohol. Nine barrels were broken. The crew might have smelled fumes. They may have thought the ship would explode.

Ships often used barrels made of oak. This wood can store liquid tightly.

The hatches of the *Mary Celeste* were left open. Some people thought that was to let the fumes out.

FAST FACT

Sailors found a wet mattress on the *Mary Celeste*. It had the mark of a child's body.

CHAPTER 4

ABANDON SHIP

The *Mary Celeste*'s only lifeboat was missing. The crew likely left quickly. They might have thought the ship was sinking.

Lifeboats became more common in the 1800s.

The *Mary Celeste* had water on board. There wasn't enough to sink the ship. But its pumps might have been broken.

CURSED TO THE END

The *Mary Celeste* had more problems later on. In 1885, its captain wrecked it on purpose. He tried to fool the insurance company into giving him money. His trick didn't work.

The crew relied on pumps to know how much water was inside the ship.

Without pumps, the crew could have been wrong about how much water was in the hold. Some experts believe this is the most likely explanation. But no one knows for sure.

FAST FACT

Some stories blame ghosts. They say the *Mary Celeste* is haunted.

Sir Arthur Conan Doyle wrote a famous story about the *Mary Celeste*. ▶

COMPREHENSION QUESTIONS

Write your answers on a separate piece of paper.

1. Write a sentence that explains the main idea of Chapter 4.

2. What do you think happened to the *Mary Celeste*? Why?

3. When was the *Mary Celeste*'s last logbook entry?

    A. November 7, 1872

    B. November 25, 1872

    C. December 5, 1872

4. Why did some people consider the *Mary Celeste* cursed?

    A. There were ghosts on the *Mary Celeste*.

    B. No one ever found the *Mary Celeste*.

    C. Bad things kept happening to the *Mary Celeste*.

5. What does belongings mean in this book?

It looked like people on the Mary Celeste *had left in a hurry. Most of their belongings were still there.*

    A. ways of moving quickly

    B. things people have as their own

    C. lifeboats kept on ships

6. What does evidence mean in this book?

Some people thought pirates had attacked. But there was no evidence of fighting.

    A. words written in a book

    B. ways that people talk

    C. signs that something happened

Answer key on page 32.

GLOSSARY

cursed

Having bad things always happening, often because of a spell.

fumes

Gases that are harmful to smell.

hold

The space in a ship used to carry or store things.

industrial alcohol

A strong chemical that is used to make fuel.

insurance company

A company that covers the costs when bad things happen.

investigators

People who work to try to find out the truth about something.

logbook

A book where sailors write about events that happen while a ship is sailing.

pumps

Machines that get rid of extra water. They can also show how much water is in a ship's hold.

TO LEARN MORE

BOOKS

Amin, Anita Nahta. *The* Mary Celeste *Ghost Ship*. North Mankato, MN: Capstone Press, 2022.

Loh-Hagan, Virginia. *Mary Celeste*. Ann Arbor, MI: Cherry Lake Publishing, 2018.

Peterson, Megan Cooley. *Ghost Ships: Are Ships Really Haunted?* Mankato, MN: Black Rabbit Books, 2019.

ONLINE RESOURCES

Visit www.apexeditions.com to find links and resources related to this title.

ABOUT THE AUTHOR

Kimberly Ziemann lives in Nebraska with her husband, three daughters, two dogs, and one cat. She works as a reading teacher with elementary students. While she enjoys writing books for children, her favorite activity is reading. She also loves learning new facts about history and science.

INDEX

A
Azores Islands, 8

B
belongings, 8
Briggs, Benjamin, 14–15

C
captain, 10, 12, 14–15, 25

F
fumes, 20

G
ghost ship, 7

H
hold, 26

I
insurance company, 25
investigators, 16, 18

L
lifeboat, 22
logbook, 8

P
pumps, 25–26

S
sailors, 4, 7, 14, 18, 21
sails, 7
storm, 12, 18
sword, 18

ANSWER KEY:
1. Answers will vary; 2. Answers will vary; 3. B; 4. C; 5. B; 6. C

The past is full of strange events, and some have left experts guessing. This series explores several mysterious occurrences, describing what happened, what might have, and what people still don't know.

Books in This Set

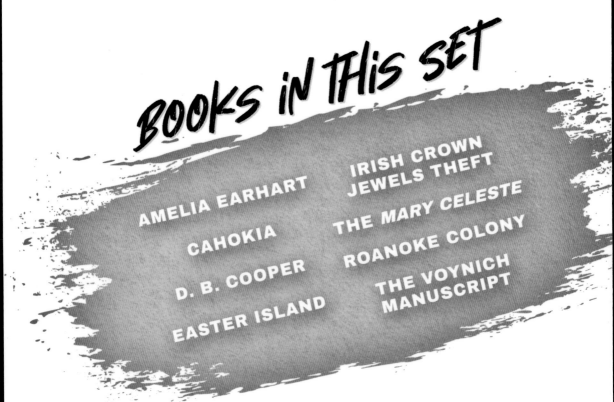

AMELIA EARHART

CAHOKIA

D. B. COOPER

EASTER ISLAND

IRISH CROWN JEWELS THEFT

THE MARY CELESTE

ROANOKE COLONY

THE VOYNICH MANUSCRIPT

Apex empowers striving readers to explore their interests with the support they need to succeed. Simple sentences and eye-catching images make each book's narrative accessible and engaging.

RL: GRADES 2–3
IL: GRADES 3–7

NOTE TO EDUCATORS
Visit **www.apexeditions.com** to find:

• Activities   • Lesson plans   • Links
• Other resources related to this title

ISBN: 978-1-63738-462-6

9 781637 384626